3-6-9 Guided Manifestation
JOURNAL

- 99 Days of Manifesting -

- By: Jessica Delvo -

GUIDED BY SPIRIT

PUBLISHING

3-6-9 Guided Manifestation JOURNAL
-99 Days of Manifesting-

Jessica Delvo

Published by Guided by Spirit Publishing

Guided by Spirit Publishing
203 Main St.
Williston, ND, 58801, USA
www.guidedbyspiritpublishing.com
info@guidedbyspiritpublishing.com

Guided by Spirit Publishing
203 Main St.
Williston, ND, 58801, USA

The information in this book is provided for informational purposes only. The author and publisher make no representations as to the accuracy or completeness of any information in this book and are not liable for any errors or omissions or for the results obtained from the use of such information.

ISBN: 979-8-9913133-0-8

Printed in the United States of America

Cover Design by Jessica Delvo

INTRODUCTION

This journal is your secret weapon for unlocking the magic of the 3-6-9 manifestation method, helping you bring your top three dreams to life in just 99 days!

Get ready to be blown away! You'll choose one powerful manifestation and then dive into the fun of writing it down 3 times in the morning 6 times at midday, and 9 times before bed for 33 days.

Sounds overwhelming? Don't be. This journal is packed with tips, exercises, affirmations, and prompts to keep your journey focused and fun. Track your progress, gain crystal-clear clarity on your goals, and feel the excitement as your dreams come to life.

Focusing on one epic manifestation at a time and journaling three times a day can lead to amazing results in 99 days or less! Stay motivated, balanced, and ready to create your dream life with this awesome journal.

Why wait? Start your magical journey to living your best life today!

Best of Intentions!

Jessie Delvo

Happy Manifesting!

4 SIMPLE STEPS

1. Set your desired manifestation

2. Write it down and journal about every day

3. Act with purpose and enthusiasm

4. Track and reflect on your progress

ABOUT THE AUTHOR:

JESSICA DELVO
Author and Master Manifester

Jessica resides in Western North Dakota with her loved ones. She is the proud owner of a marketing firm known as The Creative Dove.

Certified in meditation, she has a deep appreciation for life and is a self-taught expert in the art of manifesting.

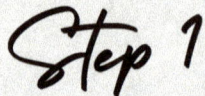 **Step 1** ....

DETERMINE YOUR MANIFESTATION AND PHRASE IT CLEARLY.

The key to this manifestation process is to get super clear about what you want and say it in a positive way.

Here's a fun formula to follow:
1. Kick off your manifestation with gratitude
2. Add in the feels (how you want to feel)
3. Use the phrase "into my life"
4. Keep it short and sweet—so you can read it in 15-17 seconds

For example:

"I'm so grateful for the universe bringing a loving and supportive relationship into my life. I feel cherished and connected. Every moment is more joyful and meaningful. Thank you!"

"I'm so thankful for the universe helping me land a job I love, filling my life with abundance, financial freedom, security, and fulfillment. I love my work and look forward to each day. Thank you!"

"I'm so grateful for the universe driving massive growth and momentum in my business, filling my life with purpose, creativity, and success. I connect deeply with my audience, they love my offers, and I enjoy financial abundance and security. Thank you!"

Step 1: Choose your manifestation and phrase it perfectly.

Step 2

WRITE YOUR MANIFESTATION DOWN MULTIPLE TIMES A DAY FOR 33 DAYS

Write it down and journal about it 3 times in the morning, 6 times at midday, and 9 times before bed for 33 days.

As you write, focus on the feelings and emotions your desired manifestation brings. Close your eyes and visualize having what you desire as if it already exists. Embrace the energy of what you want to attract.

Finally, release your desire and trust that you will receive what you asked for.

 **Step 3**

ACT WITH INSPIRATION FOR 33 DAYS.

The 3-6-9 method involves more than just journaling and visualizing—taking inspired action is crucial too. Once you clearly define the outcome you want, the universe will start sending signs, opportunities, and people to aid your manifestation.

Trust your intuition and follow the steps that excite and inspire you. Take daily actions, no matter how small, that align with your desired outcome.

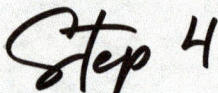 **Step 4**

TRACK & REVIEW YOUR PROGRESS

At the end of each day, spend a few moments reviewing your progress and expressing gratitude for how things are aligning and your manifestation is becoming reality. Celebrate every victory, big or small, to boost your vibration and stay in sync with the universe.

By tracking your progress, you'll see how different actions influence your results, allowing you to adjust your approach to reach your goal more effectively.

ACT WITH INSPIRATION FOR 33 DAYS.

- Write your manifestation as if it's already happening.
- Practice daily gratitude and mindfulness.
- Believe in your ability to achieve your desires.
- Be open to receiving.
- Stay adaptable and let go of fixed expectations.
- Maintain positive thinking, especially during challenges.
- Take inspired action every day for real results.
- Track your progress to stay motivated and encouraged.
- Celebrate every victory, no matter the size.
- Strengthen your faith in the universe's ability to fulfill your desires.
- Dedicate time each day to manifesting and visualizing.
- Connect with a manifestation community for extra support.
- Keep an open mind and trust that the outcome will be just right.
- Enjoy the process and stay focused on your goals!

HOW TO AVOID SELF-SABOTAGE

- Don't focus on the how of manifestation
- Don't give up, no matter how difficult it may seem to get what you want
- Avoid overthinking and stress about the outcome
- Avoid comparing yourself with others — everyone is on their own journey
- Let go of fear, doubt, and negative thoughts
- Don't ignore your intuition and inner guidance
- Avoid feeling ashamed or embarrassed about wanting or having what you desire
- Don't be afraid to ask for help when needed
- Release attachment to the outcome — trust that the universe will deliver perfect timing
- and perfect solutions
- Don't give up, even when things seem to move slowly or not at all
- Don't focus on the lack of what you want to manifest, but instead focus on abundance
- Don't get discouraged when things don't happen in the timeframe you desire
- Don't allow fear or doubt to take over — push through anyway!

33

POWERFUL JOURNAL PROMPTS TO HELP YOU MANIFEST

•••••••••••••••••••••••••••••••••••••

Use one of these journal prompts daily throughout each of the three 33-day manifestation cycles in this journal to help clear obstacles and speed up your manifestation process.

WHAT WOULD IT FEEL LIKE TO BE LIVING MY DESIRED REALITY?

_____

_____

_____

_____

_____

_____

HOW AM I HOLDING MYSELF BACK FROM MANIFESTING WHAT I DESIRE?

_____

_____

_____

_____

_____

_____

JOURNAL

IN WHAT WAYS CAN I STAY FOCUSED AN MOTIVATED IN MANIFESTING MY GOALS?

_____

_____

_____

_____

_____

_____

_____

WHAT ACTION CAN I TAKE TODAY TO MOVE CLOSER TO MY DESIRED OUTCOME?

_____

_____

_____

_____

_____

_____

_____

_____

JOURNAL

WHAT WOULD IT LOOK LIKE IF I HAD ALREADY MANIFESTED WHAT I WANTED?

_____

_____

_____

_____

_____

_____

HOW CAN I STAY PRESENT AND IN THE MOMENT WHILE MANIFESTING?

_____

_____

_____

_____

_____

_____

JOURNAL

WHAT LIMITING BELIEFS AM I READY TO LET GO OF TODAY?

_____

_____

_____

_____

_____

_____

_____

WHAT DO I NEED TO FEEL SAFE, SECURE, AND CONFIDENT AS I MANIFEST?

_____

_____

_____

_____

_____

_____

_____

JOURNAL

WHAT UNIQUE SKILLS AND TALENTS DO I POSSESS IN MANIFESTING MY DESIRES?

_____

_____

_____

_____

_____

_____

WHO ARE THE PEOPLE THAT CAN HELP ME MANIFEST MY GOALS QUICKLY AND EASILY?

_____

_____

_____

_____

_____

_____

_____

HOW CAN I BOOST MY CONFIDENCE WHILE TAKING INSPIRED STEPS TOWARD MY DESIRED OUTCOME?

_____
_____
_____
_____
_____
_____
_____
_____

WHAT ARE MY STEPS I NEED TO TAKE TO MANIFEST?

_____
_____
_____
_____
_____
_____
_____
_____

WHAT ARE MY NEXT STEPS I NEED TO TAKE TO MANIFEST MY DESIRES?

_____

_____

_____

_____

_____

_____

HOW DO I NEED TO SHIFT MY THOUGHTS, BELIEFS, AND ACTIONS TO ATTRACT MORE ABUNDANCE INTO MY LIFE?

_____

_____

_____

_____

_____

_____

_____

HOW CAN I CREATE AN ENVIRONMENT THAT WILL SUPPORT MY MANIFESTATION?

_____

_____

_____

_____

_____

_____

_____

_____

_____

WHAT ARE THE BLOCKS AND BOUNDARIES I NEED TO REMOVE IN ORDER TO MANIFEST MY DESIRES?

_____

_____

_____

_____

_____

_____

_____

_____

_____

JOURNAL

HOW CAN I KEEP AN OPEN MIND AND TRUST THAT THE UNIVERSE WILL PROVIDE THE PERFECT TIMING AND SOLUTIONS FOR ME?

_____

_____

_____

_____

_____

_____

_____

WHAT CAN I DO TO STAY FOCUSED AND ON TRACK WITH MY DESIRED OUTCOME?

_____

_____

_____

_____

_____

_____

_____

WHAT DO I NEED TO BELIEVE ABOUT MYSELF IN ORDER TO REACH MY GOALS FASTER?

_____

_____

_____

_____

_____

_____

_____

HOW CAN I REMAIN POSITIVE WHEN FACED WITH CHALLENGES AND SETBACKS IN MANIFESTING?

_____

_____

_____

_____

_____

_____

_____

_____

JOURNAL

WHAT NEW HABITS DO I NEED TO CREATE IN ORDER TO ALIGN MYSELF WITH MY DESIRED OUTCOMES?

_____

_____

_____

_____

_____

_____

_____

HOW CAN I PRACTICE GRATITUDE FOR WHAT I HAVE NOW WHILE CONTINUING TO MOVE CLOSER TO MY GOAL?

_____

_____

_____

_____

_____

_____

_____

_____

JOURNAL

HOW WOULD IT FEEL IF I HAD ALREADY ACHIEVED MY GOALS?

_____

_____

_____

_____

_____

_____

_____

WHAT CAN I DO TO BE MORE MINDFUL AND AWARE OF THE MANIFESTATION PROCESS?

_____

_____

_____

_____

_____

_____

_____

JOURNAL

WHAT WOULD IT LOOK LIKE IF I ALLOWED MYSELF TO FULLY TRUST IN THE UNIVERSE AND ITS ABILITY TO MANIFEST MY DESIRES?

_____

_____

_____

_____

_____

_____

WHAT CAN I DO TO STAY CONNECTED WITH THE ENERGY OF MANIFESTATION?

_____

_____

_____

_____

_____

_____

_____

JOURNAL

WHAT'S ONE ACTION I CAN TAKE TO STRENGTHEN MY FAITH IN THE UNIVERSE'S ABILITY TO PROVIDE FOR ME?

WHAT SMALL, DAILY STEPS CAN I TAKE TO CREATE MORE POSITIVE ENERGY AROUND MY DESIRED OUTCOME?

JOURNAL

WHAT KIND OF MINDSET DO I NEED TO MAINTAIN TO ENSURE SUCCESSFUL MANIFESTATION?

_____

_____

_____

_____

_____

WHAT DO I NEED TO LET GO OF IN ORDER TO MANIFEST MORE QUICKLY?

_____

_____

_____

_____

_____

_____

HOW CAN I STAY PRESENT IN THE MOMENT AND ENJOY THE JOURNEY TOWARD MY DESIRED OUTCOME?

_____

_____

_____

_____

_____

_____

_____

HOW CAN I TAP INTO MORE PATIENCE AS I MOVE TOWARD MY DESIRED OUTCOME?

_____

_____

_____

_____

_____

_____

_____

HOW CAN I STAY IN TOUCH WITH MY HIGHER SELF AND THE UNIVERSE TO RECEIVE GUIDANCE ABOUT MY MANIFESTATION?

_____

_____

_____

_____

_____

_____

_____

_____

_____

_____

_____

_____

_____

_____

_____

_____

33

POWERFUL AFFIRMATIONS TO HELP YOU MANIFEST

• •

Use these affirmations with the journal to remind you of your manifestation power and help yourself manifest with more confidence and ease.

I Aam Affirmations ....

1. I am worthy of receiving all the abundance the universe has to offer.
2. I attract positive energy and opportunities effortlessly.
3. My desires are on their way to me now.
4. I am open to receiving all the good the universe has in store for me.
5. I am aligned with my highest purpose and my dreams are becoming reality.
6. Every day, I am getting closer to my goals.
7. I trust the universe to deliver exactly what I need, at the perfect time.
8. I am confident in my ability to manifest my desires.
9. My life is full of abundance and prosperity.
10. I am a magnet for success and good fortune.
11. I am grateful for the miracles that are unfolding in my life.
12. I am deserving of all the wonderful things coming my way.
13. I release any doubts and embrace my unlimited potential.
14. I am attracting positive people and experiences into my life.
15. I am in perfect harmony with the flow of the universe.

16. My dreams are becoming reality faster than I ever imagined.
17. I am open to receiving unexpected blessings.
18. I am surrounded by abundance and joy.
19. I am grateful for the opportunities that come my way.
20. I believe in my power to create the life I desire.
21. The universe supports me in achieving my goals.
22. I am worthy of success and happiness.
23. I attract the right people and resources for my growth.
24. My manifestation journey is unfolding perfectly.
25. I am aligned with the energy of abundance.
26. I am grateful for every step I take towards my dreams.
27. I am confident in the timing of the universe.
28. I am constantly growing and evolving towards my goals.
29. I am a powerful creator of my own reality.
30. I attract opportunities that align with my highest good.
31. I am deserving of all the success and abundance that comes my way.
32. I am in tune with the universal flow of abundance.
33. I celebrate every victory and use it as fuel for my next success.

YOUR FIRST MANIFESTATION

. . . .

Simple Steps to follow

1. Set your desired manifestation
2. Write it down and journal about every day
3. Act with purpose and enthusiasm
4. Track and reflect on your progress

FOR THE NEXT 33 DAYS:

1. Write your manifestation 3 times in the morning, 6 times at midday, and 9 times before going to bed.
2. Journal in the morning or before going to bed using one of the 33 manifestation prompts.
3. Practice your favorite manifestation affirmations that will support your efforts and give you the confidence and trust you need to manifest with ease.
4. Reflect on aligned action steps you want to take.
5. Track progress and note down any small or big wins.

Day 1

Day 1

Day 2

Day 3

Day 4

Day 5

Day 6

Day 7

Day 8

Day 9

Day 10

Day 11

Day 12

Day 13

Day 14

Day 15

Day 16

Day 17

Day 18

Day 19

Day 20

Day 21

....

Day 22

Day 23

Day 24

Day 25

Day 26

Day 27

Day 28

Day 29

Day 30

Day 31

Day 32

Day 33

YOUR SECOND MANIFESTATION

. . . .

Simple Steps to follow

1. Set your desired manifestation
2. Write it down and journal about every day
3. Act with purpose and enthusiasm
4. Track and reflect on your progress

FOR THE NEXT 33 DAYS:

1. Write your manifestation 3 times in the morning, 6 times at midday, and 9 times before going to bed.
2. Journal in the morning or before going to bed using one of the 33 manifestation prompts.
3. Practice your favorite manifestation affirmations that will support your efforts and give you the confidence and trust you need to manifest with ease.
4. Reflect on aligned action steps you want to take.
5. Track progress and note down any small or big wins.

Day 1

Day 2

Day 3

Day 4

Day 5

Day 6

Day 7

Day 8

Day 9

Day 10

Day 11

....

Day 12

Day 13

Day 14

Day 15

Day 16

Day 17

Day 18

Day 19

Day 20

Day 21

Day 22

Day 23

Day 24

Day 25

Day 26

Day 27

Day 28

Day 29

Day 30

Day 31

Day 32

Day 33

YOUR THIRD MANIFESTATION

· ·

Simple Steps to follow

1. Set your desired manifestation
2. Write it down and journal about every day
3. Act with purpose and enthusiasm
4. Track and reflect on your progress

FOR THE NEXT 33 DAYS:

1. Write your manifestation 3 times in the morning, 6 times at midday, and 9 times before going to bed.
2. Journal in the morning or before going to bed using one of the 33 manifestation prompts.
3. Practice your favorite manifestation affirmations that will support your efforts and give you the confidence and trust you need to manifest with ease.
4. Reflect on aligned action steps you want to take.
5. Track progress and note down any small or big wins.

Day 1

Day 2

Day 3

Day 4

Day 5

Day 6

Day 7

Day 8

Day 9

Day 10

Day 11

Day 12

Day 13

Day 14

Day 15

Day 16

Day 17

Day 18

Day 19

Day 20

Day 21

Day 22

Day 23

Day 24

Day 25

Day 26

Day 27

Day 28

Day 29

Day 30

Day 31

Day 32

Day 33

CONGRATULATIONS,
You Did it!

Take a moment to reflect on your journey. What have you accomplished? What goals have you reached? How have you grown and transformed along the way?

Celebrate your successes, both big and small. Acknowledge the progress you've made and the changes you've created in your life. You've put in the work, and your dedication has paid off.

Remember, this is just the beginning. Keep the momentum going and continue to manifest your dreams. The universe is ready to support you in your next adventure!

Here's to your continued success and the exciting possibilities ahead!